Beautiful Washington D.C.

Beautiful

Washington D.C.

Text: William C. Curran
Design: Patrick H. Kolb

Third Printing, Revised, April, 1984
Published by Beautiful America Publishing Company
9775 S.W. Commerce Circle
Wilsonville, OR 97070
T. E. Paul, President

Library of Congress Cataloging in Publication Data
Beautiful Washington D.C.
1. Washington, D.C.—Description—Views. 1. Curran, William C., 1921
F195.C87 917.53'04'40222 79-17658
ISBN 0-89802-101-7
ISBN 0-89802-009-3 (paperback)

Printed in the United States of America

Contents

Introduction

Washington D.C. may be the model of national capitals. ''It is the only large city in the world,'' wrote Washington sage Willard M. Kiplinger, ''devoted exlusively to government, without the leavening of other normal human occupations.'' London is one of the world's largest banking centers and its greatest deep-water port. Paris and Moscow are major centers of international trade and manufacture and lie on important navigable waterways. If any of these was suddenly to lose its governmental function, it would go right on playing a major role in the life of its nation and the world. Washington, on the other hand, except as headquarters for our Federal Government, is unimaginable.

When in 1770 Congress asked George Washington to select a site for the newly authorized federal capital ''somewhere in the vicinity of the Potomac River'' and ''not exceeding ten miles square,'' (i.e. ten miles on a side) the first President responded like the former soldier and surveyor that he was. He first did a careful and systematic reconnaissance of more than 90 miles up and down the river.Then he made his recommendation. There can be little doubt that he made the best choice. In the beauty of its natural surroundings and in its admirable accessibility, the area still works well as a national capital, even 200 years later. Nothing could have been more appropriate than Congress' naming the district for Washington.

The original grants of land from Maryland and Virginia provided the new District of Columbia with a generous hundred square miles in which to grow. By the 1840s, this seemed to be more than would ever be used and so the portion west of the river was receded to Virginia at her request. This reduced the District to its present 68 square miles, a sloping V-shaped plain between the Potomac on the west—a majestic one-mile wide at this point—and the short, but broad, Anacostia on the east.

Despite its somewhat swampy character, the site and terrain were ideally suited for the imperial capital envisioned by Pierre L'Enfant, the spirited former French military engineer appointed by Washington to help lay out the city. The Frenchman dreamed of a super-Paris or a Constantinople, a city of 400-foot-wide boulevards, of grand public monuments, vast plazas, magnificent distances, all set off by acres and acres of lavishly cultivated greenery. Before he could give form to his dream, L'Enfant ran afoul of the country's first real estate lobby. It didn't take a lot of figuring for the early land speculators to realize that the Frenchman's ambitious dimensions weren't leaving much of that hundred square miles for their tenements. Their protest was loud and strong.

At first Washington stood firm and backed his city planner. In time, however, he fired the headstrong L'Enfant just to keep peace. Happily for the nation, before the Frenchman could be ordered to roll up his steel tape, he had managed to fix his indelible stamp on the face of the city. In the 1870s, President Ulysses Grant directed Commissioner of Public Works, Alexander "Boss" Shepherd, to dust off L'Enfant's plan and finish the job as best he could. Shepherd did a whale of a job.

Although he did not live to see it, L'Enfant's plan was realized: not only his broad boulevards and grand vistas, but also the wealth of greenery he had dreamed of. Early on it must have been discovered that a startling variety of trees, shrubs, and flowers would thrive in the mild, moist climate of the Potomac basin, and many exotics were introduced into the city, often by Americans who had served abroad, or, later, by members of the large international community.

It's possible that Washington outdoes all other American cities in the amount of space given over to growing things. Officially, there are 753 parks, totaling almost 8,000 acres, ranging from giant Rock Creek at just under 2,000 acres down to playgrounds for pre-schoolers. Add to these the campuses of six universities, the National Arboretum, the spacious grounds of institutions like St. Elizabeth's Hospital, Washington Cathedral, the Franciscan Monastery, and Walter Reed Medical Center, and it's no surprise that when seen from the air in summer Washington appears as a green expanse punctuated by white buildings.

In reality, Washington has several "faces," and it is possible to use architecture to identify different parts of the city. From the Library of Congress to the Kennedy Center, and from Pennsylvania Avenue to the Potomac, the dominant structure is the massive stone building, usually incorporating some classical, renaissance, or medieval motives. North of Pennsylvania Avenue, roughly as far as Massachusetts Avenue, is "downtown," an area of white brick, concrete, steel and glass—office buildings, stores, hotels, and restaurants. This is the city's central retail and financial district. Much of the remainder of the District is residential, and if it has a characteristic structure, it is the brick row houses, especially east of the Capitol and in Georgetown. Made from iron-rich local clay, the building bricks give the houses an unmistakable appearance. The larger houses—and this would be true in Georgetown—are sometimes classics of the Federal style. Even the small ones have a special charm and often feature bay windows, cast-iron fences around tiny yards, and brick walkways shaded by small ailanthus trees.

Like most cities, Washington has its mythology: the collection of stories long-time residents like to tell about ''what it's really like'' to live there. Stories of this nature tend to consist mainly of complaints, to be sure, but in order to survive, they have to be at least partly true. A quick rundown of the things that are repeatedly said about Washington would have to include the summers, the winters, the traffic, the nightlife, and the ambience.

Complaints about the weather fall into two rather unremarkable catagories: heat and humidity in summer, cold and snow in winter. A look at the record book will show that the District, in fact, does not excel in either of the measurable aspects of summer mugginess, but on a sweltering August day, it's not much consolation to know that it's even worse in Houston, Biloxi, and Terre Haute. The snow is something else again. Washington winters are statistically mild—enough so that snow-removal equipment has never been an item in the District's budget. However, when it gets around to snowing, it snows a lot: 19 inches in one blizzard in 1979, for instance. At times like that, Washington slips and slides to a standstill.

Washington traffic is legendary, and no story of the city is complete without some mention of the Lincoln Memorial Circle. It is true that L'Enfant's grand design did not take the automobile into account, since the design—and the city—are older than the automobile by some 150 years. The trick, of course, it to know where and how you're going, but even then the pace and aggressiveness of the drivers may come as a surprise.

Comments about the nightlife have one main thrust: there isn't any. This, of course, is hard to gauge: Washington appears, at least, to have enough bars, discos and nightclubs, theater and cultural events, to accommodate the people who enjoy them. The District resident, in fact, may be inclined to think there's too much nightlife, rather than too little, but he'd be taking into account the enormous volume of official entertaining that takes place behind closed doors in the foreign embassies and private homes of officials at all levels.

It has also been said of Washington that it lacks the instantly recognizable character of a New York, San Francisco, or New Orleans. That is true, but the reason Washington isn't much like any of those places is because it's so much like itself. Anyone who has lived and worked in the capital is likely to agree that there is an unmistakable feel about the place. In some undefinable way, it is like no other city on earth. Part of it is the charm of a city where history may count for more than it does elsewhere. And some of it is the excitement that is inescapable at the seat of the world's most powerful government. But underlying the excitement and the charm is a mysterious local atmosphere of tentativeness, a sense of impermanence. This may go far back in the city's history, to an era when a shift in administration meant, in effect, a shift in population because all jobs were political. Even today, the Washingtonian is likely not to be a native.

There may never have been a time since its founding that Washington has been free of talk about moving the Federal Government elsewhere. It reached a kind of crescendo after the Civil War, when it was seriously proposed in Congress that the capital be relocated in the Mississippi Valley. Throughout the 1950s, the most unquenchable rumor in a rumor-ridden city was that the Government would be moved to Denver "to guard against atomic attack and economize on air conditioning." But lately it seems there has been an unconscious decision to forget about moving elsewhere and settle in on the banks of the Potomac forever. It's about time, too, because neither the Government nor anyone else is likely to find a prettier or more pleasant place to do business.

School-Trip Washington

In the years immediately following World War II, one of the Washington papers could be counted on to run a late-winter news-story with a headline like: "Capital Braces. Estimate Two Million Visitors." Maybe the figure was only one million; whatever it was, at the time, it seemed like a great many. Today the capital handles more than 20 million a year and the figure is still rising. Buried among these millions is that loyal core of springtime high school excursionists; college students; and the American familes—the bulk of the visitors—and an increasing number of foreign visitors. It's a good bet that virtually the entire 20 million will return home even more enthusiastic than when they came. The reason is obvious. Washington is just about the most broadly enjoyable destination in the history of travel.

For anyone who is intellectually curious, the capital can be endlessly fascinating. In the two and a half miles separating the Folger Shakespeare Library on Capitol Hill from the Kennedy Center for the Performing Arts, overlooking the Potomac, there may be more engrossing sights and activities than in any comparable stretch in the world. Even if the curious visitor didn't read a single book from the 11 million at the Library of Congress, his lifetime might be consumed trying to have a look at the 60 to 70 million items in the custody of the Smithsonian Institution, or the 100 thousand art objects at the National Gallery, or rummaging in the millions of records in the National Archives. Fatigue, or old age, would set in long before he got to the top of the Washington Monument, toured the White House, saw the population "clock" at the Department of Commerce, or heard a concert at the Kennedy Center.

The best advice to the visitor is to stroll around a bit, and see the city from the outside before plunging into its museums, galleries, and public buildings. In fact, a walk down The Mall from the Capitol to the Lincoln Memorial is probably a good prescription for cooling the senses and getting accustomed to the scale of the place. The broad marble steps of John Russell Pope's National Gallery, or the edge of the Reflecting Pool, or the steps of the Lincoln Memorial itself invite resting and contemplation. A return route up the south side of The Mall will take the stroller past its oldest completed structure, the red sandstone "castle" of the Smithsonian. Back on Capitol Hill—simply "the Hill" in Washington talk—the visitor is sure to have a deepened appreciation of L'Enfant's "noble prospect" as he looks westward over The Mall toward the Virginia Hills.

Before the air age, most visitors were introduced to the nation's capital as they stepped from the darkness of the lovably cavernous old Union Station into the Plaza. Few thrills can match that first sudden sight of the great white dome of the Capitol looming above the trees, the noise of the cars and taxis around the Columbus Monument Circle. The visitor finds himself at the hub of the nation's business. A five minute walk would see him shaking hands with one of his Senators at the Senate Office Building just across the Plaza; another five and he could be standing in the Capitol Rotunda.

With a multi-million dollar face lift, the old Union Station has been converted into the National Visitor Center. A sleek new Union Station has been built just yards behind it. The visitor has merely to detrain and walk through the Visitor Center to the Plaza.

In Washington, all things seem to relate to the Capitol. Streets radiate from it, dividing the city into quadrants. Even taxi fare zones are measured from the Hill.

The original design for the Capitol came from an amateur architect, Dr. William Thornton. The building was constructed in fits and starts, burned by the British in 1814, and not really finished until 1863, when T.U. Walter's 16-million pound cast-iron dome was raised over the original. Maybe we dare not think of the Capitol as finished yet. In the 1950s, Congress ordered the East Front enlarged and refaced with marble, and some members are beginning to eye the West Front. Inside the Capitol, there is a lot for the visitor to see—House and Senate chambers, committee meetings, statuary, murals, inscriptions, and the senate subway.

The visitor may welcome the brisk walk across the East Capitol Plaza to reach the severely classical, white marble front of the Supreme Court Building. The Court has occupied part of the Capitol through most of its history, and when it got its own building in the 1930s, it seemed natural that it would be on the Hill. Inside, architect Cass Gilbert's building is rich in marble, heavy wood paneling, thick carpeting, and velour trappings. The solemn, muffled atmosphere makes plain that some weighty thinking goes on behind those heavy doors. The great spiral staircase is a surprise feature and its elliptical curves help soften somewhat the building's angular severity.

Immediately south of the Court building is the green-domed Library of Congress, whose priceless contents make up for its Renaissance architecture. In contrast, the studied absence of decoration from the attractive Annex—appropriately named for Thomas Jefferson—helps strike a startling balance between the two as they face each other across 2nd Street S.E. Congress' own library has grown into the world's largest and it has custody of 100 million items—housed in 12 buildings—with no end in sight. The new Madison Building, south of the Capitol, will help ease the pressure for space. All this grew from Jefferson's personal library—6,000 volumes—which he sold to Congress after its collection had burned.

In a city of libraries—100 at last count—the Library of Congress is breathtaking in its comprehensiveness. Its reference service—established for the convenience of Congress, but available to all—has no equal. Within the building, the rococco marble staircase, and the central reading room are indoor landmarks. The "Library" is not all books. Its Coolidge Auditorium presents some of the best classical music in town.

No person of literary interests should leave the Hill without taking in the Folger Shakespeare Library. Although the library is administered by Amherst College, benefactor Henry Clay Folger wisely directed that it be built in the highly accessible national capital. In addition to housing one of the world's greatest collections of English literature and Shakespeareana, the Folger has a usable replica of an early 17th century London theater and exhibits of Elizabethan life and customs.

As the visitor descends from Capitol Hill to The Mall, the first attraction he will encounter is the U.S. Grant Memorial. Among the District's statuary, the Grant Memorial is the biggest, with lots of bronze Union troopers and snorting horses attending the Commanding General (Grant was the Army's finest horseman). One of the best of the many equestrian statues that decorates Washington's traffic circles is Gutzon Borglum's fighting Phil Sheridan. Among the most moving (and nonequestrian) is Felix deWeldon's Marine Corps Memorial in Arlington. The recent trend in memorials is toward abstraction like the Robert Taft Memorial.

Dominating the east end of The Mall is the white marble expanse of the National Gallery of Art, flanked by its brand new, triumphantly modern East Wing. Sometimes still called the Mellon Gallery after its first benefactor, Andrew Mellon, the National has grown in its less than fifty years into one of the world's most important art museums. Traditionally, its immense collection has run toward old masters and Europeans. This policy is rapidly changing, especially with the advent of the East Wing, which features a giant Calder mobile and some spectacular contemporary outdoor sculpture.

Before he does anything else, any American leaving the National Gallery by the front should dash across Constitution Avenue to the National Archives. There, after passing through the world's largest bronze doors, he can see with his own eyes three of history's most important documents, the Declaration of Independence, the Constitution, and the Bill of Rights. Elsewhere in the building there are enough documents, microfilm, and curios to satisfy 200 years of snooping. But these three are the most significant.

It's hard to define the Smithsonian Institution. Known affectionately as "the nation's attic" it is part museum, part archive, part art gallery, part publishing house, part science lab, part zoo, part theater, part concert hall, and much more. The Smithsonian has varying degrees of administrative responsibility for such diverse public charges as the National Gallery, the National Zoo, the Canal Zone Biological Area, and the Kennedy Center. Crowning the paradox, it is a private foundation, charged by the government with these many tasks and given appropriations as necessary. Founder James Smithson, illegitimate son of an English peer, suffered much neglect in his lifetime. He left half a million dollars to a classless country he had never visited to found a society for the "increase of knowledge." If Smithson sought immortality, he hit the jackpot. The organization he helped found now outdraws even Disneyland. In 1904, the Englishman's body was brought to the U.S. for reburial in downtown Washington. For most visitors, the red stone headquarters building, which looks like the set for a film version of Scott's *Ivanhoe*, the Natural History, and History and Technology Museums, and the National Air and Space Museum are the heart and soul of the Smithsonian and The Mall.

Esthetically, the Washington Monument may be the most satisfying structure in the capital. There is a kind of magic in the way its clean, vertical lines hover over a markedly horizontal city. At 555 feet, 5 and 1/8 inches, the most visible landmark in the capital area, the Monument is the tallest masonry structure in the world, likely never to be topped in this age of steel-girdered structures. It has nothing to fear locally from skyscrapers, because the Fine Arts Commission limits the height of buildings in downtown Washington. At one time a favorite visitor's ritual was to climb the 898 steps to the top, but this is no longer permitted. Today, everyone must take the elevator and content themselves with the challenge of reading 189 dedicatory inscriptions as they walk down.

From the Monument, the obvious place to head next is the Lincoln Memorial, located at the other end of the Reflecting Pool. The building is remarkably compact for its size, and its balance of horizontal and vertical lines complement perfectly the powerful upward thrust of the Monument and the rounded, rambling character of the Capitol, two miles distant. The addition of the Reflecting Pool proved to be a stroke of genius. There is no question, either, about the impact of its interior. The chamber containing Daniel Chester French's giant statue of a brooding Lincoln has become one of the unofficial sanctuaries of the nation.

When the Kennedy Center for the Performing Arts opened in 1971, its opera house, concert hall, and theater instantly added a new dimension to cultural life in the capital. The world's leading artists vie to play the Kennedy Center. The Center is the vision of the distinguished American architect, Edward Durell Stone. Its Grand Foyer, more than 600 feet long, is dominated by Robert Berks' controversial giant bust of the late President, and has become one of the most popular meeting places of Washington's society.

With almost 10 thousand visitors a day lined up hoping to get in, the White House must be the best known residence in the country. It became white after British incendiaries had scorched the sandstone exterior in 1814 and Congress decided it would be cheaper to paint it than to make repairs. It was not until the administration of Teddy Roosevelt almost a century later that the new title appeared on official Presidential stationery. More than the most familiar residence, the White House may be the most renovated in the country. Each President has the perogative of decorating the house as he sees fit. In Truman's administration, the insides of the building were scooped out and reconstructed, perhaps the most prodigious residential remodeling in history. The history and decor of the East Room, the Blue Room, the Oval Office, the State Dining Room, and the Lincoln Bedroom are a familiar part of the national lore.

Historic Lafayette Square across Pennsylvania Avenue from the White House was intended by L'Enfant to be the President's front yard. In proper republican fashion, George Washington scotched the idea of so much real estate being assigned to the Chief Executive, and ordered it made a public park. Through much of the city's history, the Square was its most fashionable address. Today, the Square is largely institutionalized and only Decatur House and the Dolley Madison House remain of the many historic mansions which once lined the park. St. John's Episcopal Church, "the church of the Presidents," actually faces 16th Street, but is counted in the ambience of the Square. No one is quite sure why Andrew Jackson's statue holds the center of a park named for Lafayette, while the Marquis' statue is thrust into the southeast corner. It is best seen in late spring, when the magnolias are in bloom.

No architecture buff should miss the Old Executive Office Building just west of the White House. Built in Grant's administration to house the Departments of State, War, and Navy, it is a masterpiece of late Victorian ebullience, featuring columns upon columns, dormers, chimneys, and assorted decorated gimcracks to delight the eye. Inside it is a labyrinth of tiled hallways, lined in dark wood, which lead to an abundance of high-ceilinged, dark and comfortable looking offices. Directly across Pennsylvania Avenue from "Old State" is Blair-Lee House, the nation's official guest home. Understandably, neither is open to the public.

The Work-a-day Capital

On any Monday morning, while the sightseer is still yawning in his motel room, more than 400,000 federal workers, civilian and military, are headed for their offices. They leave from red-brick rowhouses around Lincoln Park, estates in Potomac, garden apartments in Arlington, "dormitories" near DuPont Circle, stucco cottages in Takoma Park, ramblers in Silver Spring, and high-rises in Rosslyn. By the tens of thousands they stream into the Federal Triangle, the venerable, many-winged Interior Department, the Department of Labor fortress near the Capitol, Foggy Bottom's State Department headquarters, the beautifully-housed Department of Housing and Urban Development in L'Enfant Plaza, and many more.

Additional thousands travel away from the city toward the out-of-town sites favored by low-profile officialdom—to the stolid whiteness of CIA headquarters in Langley, Virginia, the glassy expanse of the NSA operations building at Fort Meade, Maryland, or the Atomic Energy Commission at Germantown, Maryland. The servants of the Republic travel mostly by private car and bus, but increasingly by the sleek new Metrorail system, which when completed will link points as distant as Laurel, Maryland, and Dulles International Airport. By the time the visitor is ready to tackle the curving exhibit halls of the Hirshhorn Museum, Uncle Sam's 400-billion-dollar-a-year business is in high gear.

The legendary Pentagon Building, the Defense Department's headquarters in Arlington, is hardly typical of federal workspace. This is all the more reason for taking a closer look. It's convenient too; just eight minutes by Metro's Blue Line from Metro Center. The parking lot holds an impressive 8,000 cars, but the Defense Department admits to having more than 22,000 workers reporting every day. Some observers think that it may be as high as 30,000, which would match the population of Maryland's capital, Annapolis. The Pentagon was begun four months before Pearl Harbor and completed by January of 1943. The 83-million-dollar price tag may have seemed outrageously high then, but the building probably could not be duplicated today for ten to 15 times that amount and certainly not in that length of time. It was not a bad price for what was to be for a quarter-century the world's largest office building. Depending upon whether you view New York's World Trade Center as one building or complex, the Pentagon may *still* be the world's largest office building. Anyway, with its 6,546,360 square feet of workspace, there can be no doubt that it is the world's largest five-story office building.

Even 36 years after its construction, the Pentagon's figures are still startling. Its 17½ miles of corridors provide its occupants access to 685 drinking fountains, 285 washrooms, 10 snack bars, and six cafeterias. The famous Concourse with its bank, post office, department store, and miscellaneous shops might do service as a shopping mall in a small town. Each section of the building's outer rings is 921 feet long. A lunchtime jog around the building would cover just about a mile.

Architect G.E. Begstrom's unusual design has proved not only functional and durable, but a bit mysterious as well. The five-story building has five concentric five-side rings, connected by ten radial corridors and surrounding a central court that measures exactly five acres. All this has raised speculation about its symbolism—the wagon train in a circle, for instance—but no one can come up with a totally convincing interpretation. In figurative language the case has been quite different. Since the business of its tenants is of some concern to people of the world who speak a hundred or so different languages, "pentagon" may be the world's most widely and immediately understood metaphor. The building's undramatic configuration has worn well with most observers over the years, and it may be that the Pentagon, along with the Washington Monument, will survive changes in taste better than most other structures in Washington.

The frequent references to Washington as "a one-industry city" or a "company town" can mislead the visitor about the true nature of the population. There's no denying that having 400,000 residents on a single payroll can create a tilt in the local economy. The real surprise in this figure, however, is that it represents only about one-fourth of the capital area's work force. Contrary to public notion, not everyone in Washington works for the Federal Government, not even indirectly. It stands to reason that Government workers need to be housed, clothed, fed, transported, made secure, lobbied, entertained, spied on, and cured of affliction, both physical and spiritual. This calls for a lot of non-Federal help. We may speculate, then, that for each Government stenographer, there is a hairdresser, a bank clerk, and a cocktail waitress; for each official in a regulatory agency, three lawyers in a private practice. There are 1,200,000 other wage earners in the metropolitan area whose work brings them only infrequently into direct contact with the activities of government.

In a curious way, a bit in the spirit of a medieval city, some of Washington's major streets attract to themselves particular activities. Massachusetts Avenue has long been ''embassy row.'' Pennsylvania Avenue has always been very much a Federal boulevard, route of Presidents and victorian armies. Connecticut is a business street—banks, offices, hotels, restaurants—in the spirit of the U.S. Chamber of Commerce, which stands at its foot. Sixteenth Street is the avenue of the national associations and, secondarily, an embassy row. Whatever L'Enfant's wishes were in the matter, the original naming of streets did not foresee a great growth. Numbering the north-south streets is an old American custom, handy because you can't conveniently run out of numbers, but lettering the east-west streets was another matter. Just as soon as the city had grown north 26 blocks, there was a problem. This was resolved for the moment by beginning a new alphabet of two-syllable names—Adams, Belmont, Chapin, etc. Progress pushed the city engineers through Upshur, Varnum, and Webster faster than anticipated and letter carriers found themselves working a third alphabet of three syllable names—Allison, Buchanan, Crittenden. A fourth alphabet was inevitable. This one took horticulteral names and mercifully the District line ended the emergency at Verbena Street.

Through its first hundred years, Washington scarcely rated a foreign embassy and not many delegations either. That's because it wasn't considered a very important capital. All that has changed. At a recent count, there were 128 of them, most clustered along Massachusetts Avenue N.W. between DuPont Circle and the Naval Observatory. The Soviet Embassy has long been at 1125 16th Street N.W. and was the closest foreign embassy to the White House until the Fiji Embassy opened on K Street. It isn't clear why Massachusetts Avenue attracted so many foreign missions, but it must have something to do with the availablity of mansions and townhouses suitable to be converted to chancelleries. The large and attractive British Embassy, just below the Naval Observatory, has long ranked as one of the showcases of embassy row. The clean design of the Venezuelan Embassy at 24th Street also draws favorable comment.

Washington has on occasion been described as a city of churches. Since there are only about 500 churches, this must refer to their architectural splendor. Washington Cathedral, the biggest, dominates the skyline of northwest Washington, partly because of its size, partly because it is one of the highest spots in the city. The National Shrine of the Immaculate Conception, near Catholic University a few miles east of the Cathedral, comes off almost as well in elevation. Looming above the thick trees in the residentail northern half of the city, the two cathedrals offer a nice balance to the skyline of public buildings in downtown Washington. The sixth largest church in the world, Washington Cathedral, is nominally Episcopalian, but it is open for use by all worshipers. It has been under construction since 1908 and is about

THE SECOND D
ION
TOULON
TROYON
BOIS
DE
BELLEAU
VAUX
OISSONS
MARBACHE
ST MIHIEL
BLANC MONT
MEUSE-
ARGONNE
THE RHINE
TO OUR DEAD
1917-1919

Iwo Jima Memorial

United States Capitol

General Andrew Jackson statue in Lafayette Square

Treasury Building

THE TREASURY DEPARTMENT

Capitol Building

The White House, south lawn, Residence of the First Family

Washington Monument

Jefferson Memorial

SWORN
WE HOLD THESE TRUTHS TO BE SELF-
EVIDENT: THAT ALL MEN ARE CREATED
EQUAL, THAT THEY ARE ENDOWED BY THEIR
CREATOR WITH CERTAIN INALIENABLE
RIGHTS, AMONG THESE ARE LIFE, LIBERTY
AND THE PURSUIT OF HAPPINESS, THAT
TO SECURE THESE RIGHTS GOVERNMENTS
ARE INSTITUTED AMONG MEN. WE···
SOLEMNLY PUBLISH AND DECLARE, THAT
THESE COLONIES ARE AND OF RIGHT
OUGHT TO BE FREE AND INDEPENDENT
STATES···AND FOR THE SUPPORT OF THIS
DECLARATION, WITH A FIRM RELIANCE
ON THE PROTECTION OF DIVINE
PROVIDENCE, WE MUTUALLY PLEDGE
OUR LIVES, OUR FORTUNES AND OUR
SACRED HONOUR.
THOMAS JEFFERSON
1743–1826

Capitol Mall

Tomb of the Unknown Soldier

Library of Congress

Memorial Amphitheater, Arlington National Cemetery

Smithsonian Institution, original building

Old Stone House, Georgetown

Tidal Basin at Jefferson Memorial

The White House at night

Washington Monument and Reflecting Pool

(Following pages) Westfront, United States Capitol

Sam Rayburn Building, United States House of Representatives

Lincoln Memorial
(Following pages) Lincoln Memorial

Botanical Gardens

Health, Education and Welfare Building

Supreme Court Building

Washington Monument

National Gallery of Art

Smithsonian Institution

(Following pages) The White House and Lafayette Square

Botanic Gardens

East view of the Capitol

United States Capitol

United States Capitol

Bartholdi Fountain

Jefferson Memorial

John F. Kennedy Center for the Performing Arts

The Great Seal of the United States, adopted in 1782